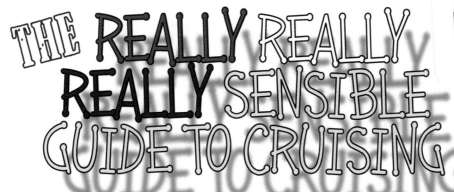

This book may be kept for

FOURTEEN DAYS

From the last day stamped below a fine of 50p will be charged for each day the book is kept over time.

22 MAY 1922			
6 JULY 1922			
12 NOV 1922			
9 APRIL 1927			
14 MAY 1928			
2 OCTOBER 1928			
30 FEB 2015			

THE REALLY REALLY REALLY SENSIBLE GUIDE TO CRUISING

Published in Great Britain by Hamborn Publishing

First published in 2014

www.hambornpublishing.com

THIS BOOK BELONGS TO

....

ABOUT THE AUTHOR

Graham Clifford is 5'10".

He was born at a young age.

He lives at home now.

Not over keen on parsnips.

For my family, friends and fan

WITH THANKS TO THE FOLLOWING PEOPLE FOR
THEIR INSPIRATION IN WRITING THIS BOOK

Abigail Taylor	Kate Walsh
Adam Davenport	Kathleen Hammond
Adam Frost	Kenny Kemp
Andrea Lach	Kerry Longfield
Andrew Chrysler	Kev Parker
Andy Fisher	Kim Bennett
Angela Brady Batty	Laura Mulley
Angela Newbery	Les Parnell
Anne Shergold-Hawkes	Leslieann Osborn
Annette Cameron	Lin Price
Becky Bryant	Lois Payne
Beryl Hampsheir	Maggie Birch
Breda Hadley	Maggie Linton
Brian Tyler	Mandy Parnell
Bridget Hope	Marci Leech
Carl Scott	Margaret Williams
Carol Hughes	Mark Stapleton
Carol Loran	Mavis Woodhouse
Catherine Morris	Mervin Wallace
Celia Jackson	Mike Litherland
Charlotte Dale	Mike Nicholas
Claire Norris	Nareen Foley
Dana Parr	Nichola Bryce
Dave Hughes	Nick Woods
Dave Watts	Nicola Malone Travelagent
Dawn Shortridge	Nigel Dyer
Debbie Hayward	Oliver Dawson
Debbie Paterson	Pat Battista
Deborah Rea	Pat Hutchinson
Denise Pilkington	Patricia Cowan
Diane Marshall	Paul Sandler
Doris Smith	Paul Traynor
Eddie Townson	Paula Louise Thomas
Elaina Marie Cutting	Pauline Deacon
Elaine Pridham	Rafal Kreft-Fryers
Ellie Price	Ruth Parker
Emma Wyeth	Sally Wimpress
Fiona M M Parker	Sandra Latham
Gail Latham	Sarah Hicks
Gail Megson	Sarah Skinner
Gayle Austin-Hogg	Sarah Smith
Hayley Harris Was Merton	Shirley Head
Iain Hayward	Shirley Townsend
Jackie Kellett	Sonia Weston
James Bavin	Steve Hedley Goonan
James Whittle	Steve Price
Jan McLeod	Steven Blackburn
Jane Matthews	Sue Fryer
Jean Thorne	Sue Litherland
Joan Bushnell	Sue Veale
John Dumencic	Sue Williamson
John Ellison	Susan Mitchell
John Ferguson	Susan Robinson
John McCourt	Tina Eshed Author
John Simpson	Tracey Quayle
Judith Fewkes Pinegar	Vanda Cowley
Judith Kitchingman	Wendy Foster
Julianne Saunders	Wendy Paterson
Julie Johnston	Wendy Taylor
Julie Ricketts	Yvonne Headford
Juliet Duffill	Zena Domaille
Karen Tyler	Zoe Bowen-Ashwin
Kate Dowling	

Demelza
Hospice Care for Children
Registered Charity Number 1039561

In association with Demelza Hospice for Children

CONGRATULATIONS!

You are about to join the growing number of people who choose to take their vacation with thousands of other passengers in a big metal boat!....Ok, let that be your first lesson, NEVER EVER CALL IT A BOAT!...It is a ship, a luxury ship, designed with every possible convenience, 5 star dining, attentive staff and decorated to the highest standard, call it a boat and you will be disowned by your fellow passengers (don't do it).

Despite it's title, this book gives you a tongue in cheek look at every step of your journey, from choosing which cruise to book, through to how to annoy people on social media with your cruise photo's when you get home.

This book is inspired by the author's experiences at sea on a range of ships and humorous observations of day to day events, and the people he has met during this time. Seen through the eyes of someone who tries to find humour in everything, prepare to go on a virtual roller coaster of rough seas and thirty foot swells, along with a mill pond like look at life at sea.

Cruise ship holidays are fantastic, relaxing and ultimately great fun, in this book we take a different look at just about everything involved in the process.

1) Find a cruise

So you've decided to book a cruise holiday this year, where do you start? Unfortunately cruise lines are very reticent to let people know about their planned cruises. It's almost like a secret society and information is passed around on a need to know basis. Very little information is available for wannabe customers, we're not sure why this is but possibly has something to do with cruise lines wanting to keep them exclusive.

So where do you start? None of the normal resources work when looking to book a cruise. There are no websites, no national advertising campaigns, travel agents know nothing about them and they certainly don't send you their expensive brochures on a day to day basis.

We sent our reporters undercover to several of the major players in an effort to find out this information for you, our findings were both shocking and a little bit scary.

After spending 4 days in a filing cabinet at Piano Cruises headquarters in Southampton, England, our slightly emaciated cruise spy, 'Agent Bob' discovered that all cruises booked in the UK go through a small Chinese laundry in Manchester. Prospective cruisers need to ask to speak to 'Maureen' and quote the coded message 'Hello Maureen, I'd like to book a cruise please'

For your benefit, we tested this theory and it actually worked (nearly), as I write, Agent Bob is currently mopping the engine room of the Isle of Man ferry.

If you are lucky enough to get through to Maureen, try not to be taken in by her lies, for the record, when we tried them, Celebrity Cruises didn't have any celebrities onboard, Princess didn't have any Princesses and Virgin don't do cruises.

In reality, once you book a cruise, you will become their No1 marketing target, their operatives will sleep on your front lawn ready to catch you in the morning, you will need to create a new email address just to cope with the sheer number of daily posts you get from them and your postman will become your worse nightmare! The photo above shows the cruise related correspondences we received in just a few days.

2) Book your cruise

So you have overcome the first obstacle, namely finding Maureen in Manchester. The next thing to think about is slightly more complicated than trying to extract the Higgs Boson particle from a comet orbiting a distant (as yet unnamed) sun.

There are many things to consider:

Where to cruise?

What ship?

Departure point?

Fly cruise?

Adult only?

Children only?

How much?

How much what?

Money of course

Oh yes, I see now

Time of year?

Ports?

So you see what started off as an idyllic idea of sipping a white wine spritzer on the prom deck has now become a bit more daunting.... (BTW, spritzer didn't come up in the spellcheck..how bizarre?)

Where to cruise?...Go to the Med, it's nice. (other destinations are available)

What ship?...Most of them have cabins (another no no!...They are called staterooms) Some are big ships, some are not quite so big. On a big ship, you can bump into someone in the embarkation terminal and not see them again (which can often be a relief). On a small ship you tend to see everyone more often throughout the course of the cruise, it's down to personal preference really, I've had plenty of people suggest that I should stay on the larger ships which is nice.

Departure point?...This of course depends on whether you are flying to pick up a ship in another country of course. The main cruise port in the UK is Southampton (until the completion of the Bristol/Swindon cruise canal in 2022) Southampton is, with a doubt, a city. Accessed by major motorways such as the M3 and M27. The city has a great deal of parking for the ships and it's football team, ironically also called Southampton is famous for winning the FA Cup in 1976 when Bobby Stokes scored the winner in the 83rd minute during the 1 - 0 defeat of Manchester United. Little known fact, Maureen played on the right wing during the match...

Fly cruise?...Nothing is more refreshing than being crammed into an impossibly small seat on one of the flying tubes after setting the alarm for 3.00am, loading your luggage into your car, driving 60 miles to the airport, standing in a queue for 2 hours, having all your toiletries confiscated including that 400ml bottle of Red Door by Elizabeth Arden that cost more than the cruise, going through customs at the other end after a full body search, worrying about getting to the port in time before the ship leaves after all of your luggage has been sent to Innsbruck. Alternatively...jump on at Southampton, Miami or wherever.

Adult Only?...This is a myth, adult only cruises do not exist. You only need to stand by reception on an 'adult only' cruise to realise that kids somehow manage to get onboard, admittedly some of them will be in their late 70s but never the less, they are in fact more whiney and immature than many 5 year olds. Main whines are 'Why hasn't my inside cabin got a window?', 'Why is it such a long walk from the dining room to the theatre?' And 'Why doesn't the shop stock Readers Digest?.

Children Only?...Don't be daft.

How much?...Your budget may not directly affect the cruise you book, many last minute deals are available and these are a great way to upset your dinner companions. Generally speaking though the larger your budget the better. Life on a cruise ship is pretty much the same for everyone, a premier suite with it's own butler and helicopter pad is fine, but outside of your suite you are the same as everyone else - unless you wear one of the increasingly popular badges that are now available to elite members:

Time of year?...Once again, this is personal choice. If you want to top up your tan, you would be better to avoid the Baltic in December, you may get a slight tint in the Mediterranean but for proper sun, head for the Caribbean. This will most likely involve flying but some cruise lines do offer departures from the UK. The Christmas markets in St Vincent are not to be missed and the Winter Wonderland park in Bermuda is a sight to see. Father Christmas himself has a condominium in Cuba and can regularly be seen spear fishing on his 25 foot motor boat 'The Grinch'

Ports?...Some people cruise for the ship experience, some cruise for the wonderful excursions available at different stops on the trip. Europe has some fantastic locations, some of them have churches and some sell ice cream. You can walk the circuit at Monte Carlo, trace the steps of Julius Ceaser in Rome or go for the whole pickpocket experience in Las Rambles in Barcelona. You can often save money by avoiding the ships excursions and experience the destinations by yourself, be aware though, the ship won't wait for you, many is the time I have had to chase the ships around Europe by planes & trains after arriving late back at the port. (I'm lying)

4) Travel to your ship

After all, it's not going to travel to you is it? The idea of a 150,000 ton floating city travelling around London's North Circular to pick you up from South Woodford is an interesting one, but I can't see any cruise line paying the London congestion charge for that and the North Circular can get very busy of course.

Maybe better then that you travel to the port of choice and board the ship there. Many options are open to you, you can travel by car, mini cab, coach, train or in extreme circumstances, a tuk tuk (not recommended)

Travelling by car is a good way of getting to the terminal, you can take as much luggage as you can fit in your vehicle and you are in charge of your own destiny. The only real problem that you will encounter is where to park. Plenty of parking is available at the docks but you could probably buy a world cruise with the money you will spend, not only that but it's not unusual for the car parking operatives to play dodgems with your cars and quite often, sell them on Ebay.

Another option is to find a local hotel for the evening before your cruise, many offer a car parking service and the combined cost can be roughly the same as just the parking fees at the docks. This is a relaxing way to start your holiday, simply get up the next morning and either get a cab or the hotel may offer a shuttle service to your ship. Word of warning here though, the hotels in Southampton for example, can be booked up years in advance as some cruisers book the hotel first before deciding on a cruise, these people are the same ones who you will see filling up their drinks bottles with juice from the buffet - more about them later.

Coach travel is popular with many passengers, most of these come long distances from the top of the UK and speak in strange dialects which, whilst being a form of English is completely unintelligible to those from the home counties. There are some limits on luggage with this form of transport and there is the possibility that you will spend 5 hours stuck with a coach load of tone deaf Geordies singing 'The fog on the Tyne is all mine all mine, the fog on the Tyne is all mine' Fortunately these same people are blessed with a fantastic sense of humour...

Tuk Tuks waiting at Southampton Ocean Terminal

5) Embarkation

So you have successfully made it to your terminal, your luggage is on it's way to your stateroom and you have been directed to the holding area where you will be processed by the wonderful smiling ladies who are there to ensure a swift, easy boarding for you. Well that's the theory.

In reality, attempting to board your ship can be labourious, tedious and other words ending with ious. After initially having your photo and fingerprints taken for your cruise card, you join a long and winding queue. Things are still upbeat, after all, you are going on holiday and everyone is excited. It doesn't take long however for anyone's patience to be tested by screaming children, flatulent grannies and the queue comedian in the Panama hat. This snaking queue repeatedly doubles back on itself but the boredom is easily defeated by said comedian shouting 'Oh hello again' every three minutes.

Eventually you will reach the security checkpoint, now of course this is a necessary evil that is required to keep the likes of Noel Edmonds, Alan Carr and Tony Blair off of the ship, but the process could be easier...you are asked to put all your bags, mobile phones, keys laptops, children etc through the X ray machine whilst Stephen from Fareham messes around on Facebook on his monitor screens. This obviously is a serious issue and is not to be joked about. Particularly after the rather infamous 'Ann Summers' incident...let's not dwell on that.

By now you have got through all the security but don't put your cruise card away just yet, you still need to pass several more Krypton Factor like obstacles before you are allowed into the atrium which has been turned into a market for the day with the intention of relieving you of your wallet. Here you are forced to walk through stalls selling wine packages, tickets to the sanctuary, spa offers, coffee deals, elite dining and I'm sure I even saw a used car lot on my last cruise.

Getting 3000 people onto a ship is a huge undertaking and as you can imagine, things are pretty frantic during this time, 2 of the 4 lifts are out of order and you have a laptop case over your shoulder, a dozen bottles of wine, and a personal holdall that you didn't trust the porters with. You struggle up 10 flights of stairs, waddle 100 yards down what seems to be an impossibly narrow corridor only to discover that you are on the wrong side of the ship. You turn around, trip over cases parked outside other peoples staterooms, cross the ship where the lifts are and at the point of collapse, you reach your room. Laden down with all your carry on items, you then need to find your cruise card/door key to let you finally relax. After checking all your pockets you remember your card has been gripped between your front teeth for the past 30 minutes, you put your card in the slot but for some reason the little light flashes red, you take it out, turn it around and try again, nothing, flip it over...nothing. Now far from being on a relaxing cruise, steam is coming out of your ears, your arms are falling off and a nagging voice behind you is telling you that you are doing it wrong, by now, fuming you accost Melvin who is busy depositing the cases outside other cabins and tear into him because after all, it's all his fault! Melvin is used to this of course because it happens at every turnaround and asks to look at your cruise card and boarding documents, he then tells you, without a hint of sarcasm that in your excitement, you have walked up one floor too many and that your stateroom is on the floor below.

6) Your stateroom

These hutches come in several forms, from the inside family room which accommodate up to 4 people in a bunk formation, right up to Deluxe Executive Multi-floor hutches with built in butlers.

Basically, your hutch is just somewhere to lay your head, store your cloths and cure your hangovers. How long you will spend in your room probably depends on how nice it is, if you've spent thousands of pounds on a suite, you need to get your money's worth, not only will this give you some much wanted peace, it will save your fellow passengers from your constant chirping about how rich you are.

INSIDE STATEROOM

OUTSIDE STATEROOM WITH BALCONY

EXECUTIVE SUITE

All rooms come with an en-suite 'bathroom' although that description is pushed to the limit in the smaller rooms, where a bath would actually be bigger than the whole room itself. There are some advantages to having a smaller room of course, you can turn on the shower without getting out of bed, it is difficult for your cabin steward to hide the TV remote (a game they like to play) and you can use words like 'bijou'.

7) Your cabin steward

Cabin stewards are a unique breed of industrious people who are on call 24 hours a day to cater for your every need. Fancy a Ceaser Salad at 3.00am? Not a problem, just reach for the phone and your snack of choice will be delivered to your room before you have put the phone down.

His duty is to maintain your stateroom, clean, 'tidy', turn your bed down, lovingly place chocolates on your pillow every night and laugh at your underwear which you left in a growing pile in the corner of the room.

It is a well documented fact that cabin stewards have evolved into a unique species of human that don't require any sleep or sustenance, I'm reminded of Jacob, a cabin steward by day, ship's navigator by night and guest entertainer in the theatre in between. Not only that but he piloted the tender, drove the coach to Seville, cooked lunch, taught us flamenco and sold souvenirs before returning to the ship to clean his allotted 250 staterooms. He was good, but not Superman by any means, I remember he was late turning down our bed that night - bit shoddy really.

By far the most important responsibility that your steward has is making towel animals. These can range from elephants to swans and THE MONKEY, which is probably responsible for 95% of cardiac arrests suffered on a ship, hanging down from the air conditioning vent above the bed, these creatures are commonly used when head office realises that they have over-booked the cruise and that 200 more people are due to board the ship in Cadiz.

ELEPHANT

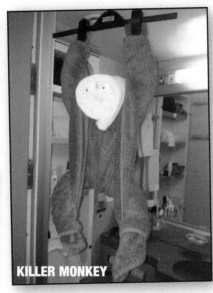
KILLER MONKEY

LOVE SWANS

CHER

QUITE DISTURBING MONKEY

CRAB

STINGRAY

RABBIT

8) Dining

Dining on a cruise ship can, and should be a culinary experience of the highest order, restaurants cater for every taste with 5 star dining in luxurious settings, options for dining are as follows:

Main Dining Rooms (MDR)... These are the focal point for a fantastic gourmet experience. You may be on a table for 2, 6, 8 or 10. If you are on a fixed dining time, you will share at least two hours each evening being attentively served by your waiters and wine waitress. If you have chosen to be social and have a table with 6 or more diners, you can share your days experiences, marvel at the scintillating conversation such as 'It's a bit rocky tonight', 'Did you have a good day?' 'Did you see the comedian last night?, he was so funny'

The waiters in the MDR are the elite, the best of the best, they passed their waiter courses by running up and down the Brecon Beacons with 200lb ruck sacks on their backs on dark January nights through wind, rain sleet and snow, these are hard men - you cannot upset them. They are ruthless, and have such incredible memories that on a table of twelve, they won't even need to write your orders down. A few minutes after taking your order they will bring your entire tables starters, and if he gives you a Chocolate love boat supreme as a starter, don't argue, that must be what you ordered...he doesn't get it wrong.

The Opulent dining room on The Independence of the Seas

Dress code in the MDR is very strict, in so much as you must conform with the dress code of the day, deviate from this, even a little bit and although the restaurant manager may overlook it, your fellow passengers will not. You will become a pariah, an outcast and will possibly be asked to go and sit by yourself. (this has happened to me on more than one occasion)

There are alternatives to the MDR, many people choose to eat in the buffet, which has been transformed into a nice option to the formality of the dining rooms. This transformation which happens almost effortlessly is achieved by a whole host of waiters, engineers and interior designers who come together every evening to 'turn the lights down a bit'.

In the buffet you will meet (whether you want to or not) interesting characters who 'can't be bothered with all that dressing up' The conversation can be every bit as interesting as 'down stairs' with wonderful oratory tales of how 'we don't like nice food', 'we don't like drink', 'we don't like cruise ships' and 'we don't like fun, we tried fun once didn't we Derek - we didn't like it'

There is of course a much wider choice of food in the buffet, but always worth bearing in mind that suspiciously, the menu in there is pretty much the same as the menu in the MDR from the evening before - make your own conclusions...

HORIZON COURT - BUFFET ON P&O's AZURA

The very best food of course, is saved for the elite deluxe dining, most ships these days take advantage of their captive audience by offering a seven star gastronomic wonderfulment (is that even a word?) dining experience. Tied in with the worlds best chefs such as Marco Pierre White, James Martin, Atul Kochhar and Ian Beale from Eastenders. There is a supplement to pay for this service, however it is a relatively small price to pay for fantastic food and is still a fraction of the price you would pay in London, New York or Walford.

Michelin-starred Atul Kochhar's Sindhu Restaurant on P&Os Azura

9) Entertainment

As you would expect, with thousands of people on a ship, they are going to need entertaining, leave them to their own devices and there would be carnage. So how do you fill the time between meals? The answer is simple, make them play bingo.

To the uninitiated, playing bingo on a ship is second only to the towel monkeys in the fatality stakes. Dedicated players will queue for hours for their tickets, some playing as many as 144 tickets per game. These are professionals, with intense powers of concentration that defies even the most ardent waiter asking 'Would you like a drink Sir...sorry, Madam. Prizes range from just a few pounds up to the cruise jackpot which can be thousands. As jackpot night draws nearer, the intensity increases and tempers get shorter, if a newby wins just a line on the first game for £14, the moaning begins and the atmosphere becomes very dark. As the evening progresses and the tension increases still further, Charlene pops along to the lounge for the first time, and wondering what all the fuss is about, buys a solitary ticket for the jackpot game...moments later, the game begins, people are severely scolded for talking, absolute silence is a must, the tension grows even more and the ship's security staff, on a code yellow alert assemble by the doors. The £1400 prize must be won tonight, Doris from Peckham is getting close, just needing two little ducks for a fortune that will almost pay her bar bill....all the fours, Forty four, the White Star line, Twenty nine, seven and one - 'BINGO!', HOUSE!' 'ERE!' Amazingly Charlene at her first ever attempt at cruise ship bingo has won the big one, a stunned disbelief filters across the room...the calm before the storm, seconds later all hell breaks loose. Sam from the ents team who was calling the numbers gets thrown clean across the room, glasses get broken, furniture up turned and a ships general alert is sounded. Calm is eventually restored and poor Charlene is taken to the medical unit on deck four with severe dabber wounds. Seventy two old ladies are confined to their cabins with orders that they be disembarked at the next port of call (which is always Cadiz) Think seriously before playing bingo, it is dangerous.

Many other daytime activities are available. Yoga, dancing, art classes, port talks, guest speakers who you have never heard of, the cinema and the inevitable quizzes. The quizzes form, a major part of the holiday for some people, and are always attended by the 'quiz nerds' These people know everything and they are not afraid to use it. Question masters hate them, other participants hate them and I think the captain does too...'Yes you're clever, go and cure kippers or something'

By far the best of the entertainment is reserved for the evenings, a growing band of comedians, singers, hypnotists, jugglers and ventriloquists spend much of their lives travelling between ships at various ports in an attempt to entertain the eager audiences awaiting them. This diverse group of people know their game, they can entertain, it's what they do day in day out every week of the year. The guest entertainers will typically do two shows in an evening, normally in the ship's theatre which is, to be honest, as good, if not better than anything that you will see in the West End or Broadway. The reason for two shows is because dinner is served in two sittings, and to be honest as large as the theatres are (1200 seats) they cannot accommodate everyone at one performance. Best be early for a seat in one of these shows though, as they can get packed very quickly, elderly guests have been known to toss their zimmer frames aside and sprint the length of the ship in order to get a decent seat. Others have taken a more sensible approach:

If you should bump into one of the comedians on deck, always make his day by saying 'I saw your show last night, heard that joke about the man who was half America half Taliban* three times on this cruise so far but you told it the best' - they love that.

Don't however expect any of these performers to be the same offstage, they refuse to juggle bread rolls in the dining room, be funny or throw their voices in public although the hypnotists are always great and are the best guest entertainers ever, best ever, best ever, best ever....ahem, sorry about that, not sure why I said it.

*He was his own worse enemy

10) Ship photographers

Without meaning to sound negative, the ship's photographers can be about as welcome as a force 12 gale in The Bay of Biscay. These tricky individuals work as a pack, their den is often located in the walkway between the various show lounges, bars and theatres on the ships. Here they wait to pounce on anyone showing even the remotest interest in the snaps of them displayed on the boards that block the view of the ocean.

They are the cruise world's equivalent of nuisance phone calls at home, no sooner will you be off the gangway at a new port than these buccaneers of the sea will be all over you 'Welcome to Gibraltar guys, would you like your photo taken with a genuine Roman centurion?' or 'Welcome to Oslo, have your photo with a genuine Rock Ape?' So geography and history aren't their strongest points but they are ruthless in the execution of their art. Once you agree to have your picture taken, they will go to town, they have secured your confidence and will now try to sell you gum, chocolate, stockings and any other black market goods that have fallen off the back of a boat that week.

If you find yourself cornered by a number of the photographers, whatever you do, don't try to fight or talk your way out of it, go along with the whole photo taking drama, they wont try to take money off of you there and then so you can still get out of this sticky situation relatively unharmed. How do you do this? Simple, every time you disembark the ship, where a handy disguise. They will take your photo but will never recognise you on the ship when you are back, dressed in your finery:

We even managed to foil the photographers at dinner by implementing the disguise
ruse - our whole table got away with it....a handy tip

Please remember though, nobody is born with the ambition of being a ship photographer, they were probably quite happy taking people wedding photos, had too much drink at the reception and someone dropped the Kings shilling in their Malibu and coke, they were then press ganged into service on the high seas. At the end of the day, they are kind of human - so try to be nice to them (but hold on to your wallets).

11) ~~m&ms~~ Shops

With ships becoming larger and larger, there is naturally more scope to relieve the weary passenger of his/her hard earned money. Boutiques, duty free and general stores offer a vast array of ever changing stock to temp and titillate you into putting your onboard account into overdraft. These shops offer huge discounts on items ranging from tooth brushes, keyrings right up to the latest Tag Heuer watches....they say. A personal hate of mine, and one that I could write a whole series of books about is the extortionate price of M&M's onboard the floating shopping malls. Bearing in mind that these prices should be 'tax free' the current going rate for M&M's onboard is something akin to a Swarovsky crystal attempt to replicate the crown jewels. In a recent letter to a cruise line, I pointed out this gross injustice, and even suggested a way around the problem but the response was curt to say the least (see page 28)

If you are going to take 'advantage' of the huge discounts onboard, you are advised to get in early. Very often, the first gentleman to look for a black bow tie will get it, leaving others to desperately trying to fashion one out of the multitude of black plastic straws that adorn any drink ordered from the bar. The stock levels are low and any attempt to purchase something other than washing powder for the Laundry normally comes with the regimented response 'No, they didn't bring any onboard at Southampton (or any other home port)'

Onboard Duty Free can give you the hump

The bow tie

Every ship has it's own 'General Store' where you can buy day to day essentials such as shampoo, books, crisps (potato chips for our American cousins) and anything else you may need. Buying them is not easy, take your overpriced Snickers or Kit Kat to the counter and you will be asked for your cruise card, the shop assistant will swipe your card and then tell you that there is a problem with the till, whereby he will have to write out a three page docket (often in less than 10 minutes) that you will have to sign before you can walk out with your treat.

All the boutiques on all of the ships are run by Nikola, who, despite having a very sexy accent doesn't really understand what you are saying. Whilst being a bit cruel, this can be a constant source of amusement. 'Hello, I'd like to buy the watch in the window' - 'You vant to vatch zee vindow? 'Oh don't worry, give me a Twix' - 'A tvix?...I am on duty Sir'

12) Sunbeds

If you should ever stumble across a cruise forum on the internet, there are several subjects so controversial that they should never, ever be mentioned. Fortunately, this is a book and there is no right of reply so I shall happily confront these subjects head on.

The topic of sunbeds is a divisive one. At the start of a cruise, there are say, 3000 passengers and 2999 sunbeds. This is not a problem as, if docked at some exotic location, the majority of your fellow passengers will be ashore and the lido deck will be a pretty tranquil place to roast in the sun. The problems begin however on sea days. The photographic department will have nothing to do until the evening and quite understandably, boredom sets in.

To alleviate the dullness of a sea day, the under developed digital purveyors of frozen moments in time initiate their own version of musical chairs, using sunbeds of course. As the days go by, fewer and fewer sunbeds are available, they are not hidden however...oh no, they are tantalisingly stacked against the handrails and tied up using knots that only Captain Pugwash himself would understand. This is a constant source of amusement to them but unfortunately the captain will overlook this as it tends to stops them congregating in the staff canteen fifteen decks below.

The inevitable consequence of these pranks is anger among the would be bathers on deck. Nothing is more controversial than a sunbed, unoccupied for more than 30 minutes but reserved with a towel and a book (this book?..who knows....) It's not unknown for leathery old people to 'reserve' three or four sunbeds at different locations around the deck in order not to miss any of that days ultra violet radiation quota.

A British cruise ship - without a German in sight

A time lapse video of the sunbeds on deck is a beautiful thing to behold, with the subtlety of wild flowers, you can see the beds gently rotate on their axis in an ever desperate attempt to follow the sun around the ship until the last hardy souls abandon their daily ritual and head back to their cabins to cover themselves in lotions and potions that will ensure their hard earned suntan lasts at least three days after they get home.

13) Passengers

We live in a diverse world and it naturally follows that your cruise will be filled with people with different accents, lifestyles and beliefs. Generally you share some basic attributes with these people, you both eat and breath air...in some cases, that is where the similarity ends. Lets have a look at some of your fellow passengers:

1) The Modern Cruiser... The modern cruiser is typically aged between 25-70 and will mainly be found propping up the bars on the lido deck. Not particularly noisy, the males drink draft beer and the female of the species Pinot Grigio. They pride themselves on knowing all the waiters names. The men will spend 4 or 5 hours at the bar moaning about how his partner is sunbathing and he doesn't know how she can stay in one place for so long. The female is quite demanding, she will drag the male around the deck for half an hour before deciding which sunbed she wants. When she finds the ideal location, she instructs the male to turn the beds around so that they face the sun.

He will now be required to adjust her back rest, lay her towel down, rub sunflower oil onto her back, get her a drink and read from the onboard newspaper what is happening on that day - despite the fact that she is not going to move for the duration unless it's for food. Once she is settled, the male can now relax on his sunbed for 2 minutes before his partner asks him to go back to the cabin to get her book and reading glasses. So perhaps it's not surprising that he chooses to park himself, just out of earshot at the bar.

2) The Wanderer... These are people who never seem to settle, rarely sit down and by the end of the cruise, have probably walked about as far as the ship has travelled. They never really get into the whole 'Sun' thing and wear trousers, socks, a large brimmed hat and a woolly fleece incase the temperature should suddenly drop below 90 degrees. These are the nomads of the ship, they like to visit every nook and cranny and will probably have an online blog somewhere explaining what they have seen.

UNCATEGORIZED PASSENGERS OVERSEEING MONACO

3) The Moaners... You have met these people, even if you haven't started cruising yet. On a ship, they are in their element and this makes them extremely unhappy. They will moan about their cabin steward, the pillows, shower, buffet, dinner, tea, bars, loungers, pools, smokers, non smokers, captain, navigator, entertainment, sea conditions, waiters, shops, prices, ship and other people. These people don't really like anything, they are only on a cruise because they read about people moaning about them in the Daily Mail so they thought they would give it a go. These people are the cruise ship version of the Dementors in Harry Potter, they will suck the very life out of a cruise and regularly turn the entertainment team into a suicidal bunch of nervous jellies who question their very existence. Let's move on, they are getting me down...

4) The Fun Fun Funsters... Even WORSE than the Dementors are this small, yet significantly noisy group of individuals who think they are part of the entertainment team. Always jolly, they will go out of their way to attract attention, especially on sailaways when the audio/video crew are on deck filming for the cruise DVD. On these occasions they can be seen shouting the words to Rule Britannia and waving the worlds biggest flag which that brought onboard for this very purpose.

14) Drinks packages

For most of us, a holiday is a time to relax, after all, you have spent a whole year with your nose to the grindstone so that you can among other things, have a two week break on a cruise ship. It goes without saying that alcohol is going to play an important part of your time onboard.

Most cruise lines offer drinks packages, these can be from simple wine packages to complete overall deals where you can drink as much as you like for roughly $45 per day. Many see the latter as a challenge. It is estimated that $45 will buy you approximately six drinks per day - but with no limit, personal record attempts are commonplace.

The sophisticate will probably opt for a nice wine package, this is a sensible option if you like wine with your meal but note, this is a limited package so filling secret drinks bottles from your table won't do you any good.

Aside from standard beer, wine and spirits, cruise ship bar staff are all accomplished cocktail makers. If you fancy a Martini, Piña Colada, Mojito or something more exotic like a Screaming Abdab or Flaming Lamborghini, these are your men. Injuries from badly shaken Singapore Slings are a rarity these days, especially since the introduction of safety netting in front of the bar. The goods news is, cocktails are included in many drinks packages.

For the benefit of the readers, I have explored some of the drinks deals available, my findings have been fuzzy to say the least.

With moony bars hic on board, it is almost impossible to avoid drinkhicing for to loong and it is easy to overdoo it early on in your cruisee woosie hic. Haha! Personally I don't drink to excess personally. I don't and as I write, I'm probably not as think as you drunk I am hic. I really love you, I doo im foheather growing bubbeeels, preety bubles in the hair, any seeen ma hat? I'm gooing to have a littel lye down now.

15) Casino

An enjoyable activity at sea is the trying your luck in the opulent casinos on the ships. These are run with ruthless efficiency with security so tight, you would think Posh & Becks were onboard.

All the usual suspects, Poker, Blackjack, Roulette and of course the slot machine are present. The slots with their flashing lights and colourful displays are designed to entice you to play, with hypnotic expertise, these machines will encourage you to insert your cruise card and tempt you to part with your money....which doesn't seem real as it's not cash (dangerous)

The casinos are of course, money making monsters and it is your job to feed them. Initially you may get lucky, win a few rounds of Blackjack, guess correctly at roulette or get ahead on the slots. This is the time to leave, for if you stay, you will be in serious need of an understanding bank manager when you get home.

You are now in a psychological war with the casino staff but you won't even know it. They won't approach you, there will be no encouragement to continue gambling but you know that you cannot stop, that big win could be just around the corner. You start to fall behind but you know this is just a temporary setback so you set limits in your mind without realising that you don't control it anymore...it belongs to the casino and you charge more and more cash to your cruise card which is being backed up by the credit card you registered when you got onboard.

After a marathon session, you are £500 down, ok, you are not going to lose your house over it but the realisation that you have lost a tidy sum of money and enjoyed doing it hits home. You feel sick and inside your head you are calling yourself all the names that you only usually reserve for the golf course. You are ashamed, and rightly so. You promise yourself that you won't be going to the casino again, you tell your partner with expert assurance that the games are all fixed, it's boring in there, and you would much rather sit on the prom deck reading a book. And that's what you do, until she goes to the Spa and you are left again to your own devices....(This is all hypothetical and certainly doesn't happen to me - no way, never)

16) Always take your lens cap off

One of the most important pieces of advice I can give you, is to always make sure that you have taken your lens cap off when taking photographs of the incredible scenery and places that you will visit. In some cases it won't make much difference to the quality of your pictures but when you have spent thousands of pounds touring Europe, it's always nice to have a visual reminder of the places you visited. I took these photos in Monaco recently after breaking the lens cap rule and you can see for yourself the difference it can make.

TUNNEL

START/FINISH LINE

CASINO SQUARE

LA RASCASSE

PANORAMIC VIEW OF MONTE CARLO

WITHOUT LENS CAP

The same picture taken with and without the lens cap on. Notice how the photograph on the left has more colour and depth of field compared to the picture on the right. This is almost entirely down to the removal of the lens cap when using the camera.

WITH LENS CAP

17) Port guides

Port is produced from grapes grown and processed in the demarcated Douro region. The wine produced is then fortified by the addition of a neutral grape spirit known as aguardente in order to stop the fermentation, leaving residual sugar in the wine, and to boost the alcohol content. The fortification spirit is sometimes referred to as brandy but it bears little resemblance to commercial brandies. The wine is then stored and aged, often in barrels stored in a cave (pronounced kahv and meaning "cellar" in Portuguese) as is the case in Vila Nova de Gaia, before being bottled. The wine received its name, "port", in the later half of the 17th century from the seaport city of Porto at the mouth of the Douro River, where much of the product was brought to market or for export to other countries in Europe. The Douro valley where port wine is produced was defined and established as a protected region, or appellation in 1756, making it the oldest defined and protected wine region in the world. Chianti (1716) and Tokaj (1730) have older demarcation but no regulation associated and thus, in terms of regulated demarcated regions, Porto is the oldest.

The reaches of the valley of the Douro River in northern Portugal have a microclimate that is optimal for cultivation of olives, almonds, and especially grapes important for making port wine. The region around Pinhão and São João da Pesqueira is considered to be the centre of port production, and is known for its picturesque quintas—farms clinging on to almost vertical slopes dropping down to the river.

Wine regions

The demarcation of the Douro River Valley includes a broad swath of land of pre-Cambrian schist and granite. Beginning around the village of Barqueiros (located about 70 kilometres (43 mi) upstream from Porto), the valley extends eastward nearly to the Spanish border. The region is protected from the influences of the Atlantic Ocean by the Serra do Marão mountains. The area is sub-divided into 3 official zones-the Baixo (lower) Corgo, the Cima (higher) Corgo and the Douro Superior.

Baixo Corgo – The westernmost zone located downstream from the river Corgo, centered on the municipality of Peso da Régua. This region is the wettest port production zone, receiving an average of 900 mm, and has the coolest average temperature of the three zones. The grapes grown here are used mainly for the production of inexpensive ruby and tawny ports.

Cima Corgo – Located further upstream from the Baixo Corgo, this region is centered on the town of Pinhão (municipality of Alijó). The summertime average temperature of the regions are a few degrees higher and rainfall is about 200 mm less. The grapes grown in this zone are considered of higher quality, being used in bottlings of vintage and Late Bottled Vintage Ports.

Douro Superior – The easternmost zone extending nearly to the Spanish border. This is the least cultivated region of Douro, due in part to the difficulties of navigating the river past the rapids of Cachão da Valeira. This is the most arid and warmest region of the Douro. The overall terrain is relatively flat with the potential for mechanization.

To summarise - it gives me a headache.

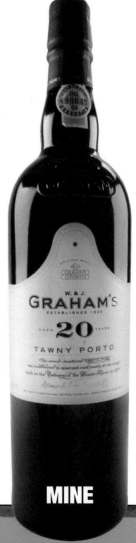

18) Port guides (sensible)

Cruise ships visit some fantastic ports throughout the world, some with magnificent history, others with outstanding scenery. We can only touch on a few of these ports, lets start at one of the most historic and beautiful - Tilbury

Tilbury in Essex, England, can be seen from Gravesend across the river Thames. Enough said...

Port of Tilbury, voted 2nd only to Felixstowe in terms of beauty - simply stunning

Living in the shadow of ports mentioned above are the less desirable docks of Valetta in Malta, Monaco, St.Thomas and Alaska.

SOMEWHERE WITH PALM TREES

ST. THOMAS

VALETTA, MALTA

ALASKA

19) Port guides (last try)

One of the best things about cruising, is that you can wake up each morning in a different country (without having been on your stag do the night before) Many are beautiful, but lots are primarily working ports filled with cargo containers. Lets look at some of the ports on a typically British cruise to the Mediterranean.

First port of call will normally be one of the Atlantic venues such as Vigo in Northern Spain, Lisbon, Cadiz or the gateway to the Med - Gibraltar:

Gibraltar is a British Overseas Territory located on the southern end of the Iberian Peninsula at the entrance of the Mediterranean. It has an area of 2.3 square miles and a northern border with the Province of Cádiz in Andalusia, Spain. The Rock of Gibraltar is the major landmark of the region. At its foot is a densely populated city area, home to almost 30,000 Gibraltarians and other nationalities.

Those are the facts, here is the nonsense: Gibraltar, or Gib as the experienced cruiser calls it isn't really a port of call at all. In reality it is a pit stop. Pit stops in Gib never take more than half a day and are used for filling up with cigarettes, booze and M&Ms at a fraction of the price than the cost onboard. Of course. the first couple of times you stop in Gib, you will do the Apes, the caves and the cable car. Having got these out of your system, you will tend to wander from cafe to cafe in the high street looking for a decent WIFI signal. Fortunately, there are plenty of these and you can happily lose a whole morning catching up on Facebook or the 300 emails that you have received since you left Southampton 3 days ago.

Be warned, Gib High Street can be very busy, apparently there is a ship in port with 3000 passengers anxious for a walk on dry land. The port here is a working one and not very pretty but the views of the rock are excellent, with a pair of binoculars you can see the apes up in the hills, the cable car, possibly some dolphins in the habour and most definitely a family from Oldham carrying 4 cases of John Smiths Bitter, 3 boxes of Walkers crisps, a box of wine and the world's largest Toblerone.

GIBRALTAR - TESCO'S OF THE CRUISE WORLD

Once you are in the Med proper, your next stop could well be one of the Italian islands, (I told my wife I was going to a fancy dress party as an Italian island once...she said 'Don't be Sicily') Which is a seamless link to let us look at the rather oddly shaped football at the bottom of Italy's boot...**Sicily**

Sicily is possibly the most beautiful island that you will ever see, once you get through the dock area which looks like the aftermath of the 100 days of 'games' at the Colosseum in the heyday of the Roman Empire.

With every cruise ship that stops in Messina, Sicily's main port, comes a titanic struggle between two of the worlds most infamous criminal organisations, the Mafia, and Betty from Redbridge. Being a bit scared prevents me from elaborating on this subject but suffice to say, street crime in Redbridge is widely regarded as being the lowest in the western world, and local businesses rarely have any trouble with theft, vandalism and arson...just saying.

Possibly your next port will be ~~Civich Cichiv Chiviteche~~ **Rome.** Rome is with a doubt, the greatest city in Europe. It has of course a wonderful history which even predates the Roman Empire. The city is full of ancient Roman buildings, The Colusseum, The Pantheon, the wonderful forum, Circus Maximus...the list goes on and on.

The Colusseum has been nearly 2000 years in the making and it looks like they are getting very close to finishing it. The roof is being built in Bristol and will be transported in one piece by sea, air, road and taxi. This really is a very impressive example of Roman ingenuity and is a must for any traveller to Rome.

The Pantheon is a classic example of how old and new mix in the eternal city, just walking through the streets of Rome and you will stumble across this magnificent building surrounded by hotels, shops and apartments. Like the Colusseum it's not quite finished as there is still a bit of a hole in the roof, proving beyond doubt that they even had cowboys in Roman times.

There is such a huge amount of history in Rome that we cannot do it justice in this book.

Apart from the enormity of the Roman Empire, the capital of the Catholic church is based in an enclave within the city. **The Vatican City**

Should you wish to visit the basilica or the Vatican museum, you are advised to join the back of the queue which starts generally in the atrium on the ship (50 - 60 mile queues are not uncommon)

Always remember before visiting the Vatican that there is a strict dress code, ladies should keep their shoulders covered and gentlemen should refrain from wearing Mankini's. Such are the wishes of the Bishop of Rome.

HOLE IN PANTHEON ROOF

Staying with Italy, we head up the coast to the ancient port of Livorno for a short coach or train journey to either Florence or Pisa. One is an absolute highlight -- the gem of the early Italian Renaissance. In the 15th century, when great artists like Giotto, Ghiberti, Brunelleschi and Michelangelo worked there, they created magnificent examples of painting and sculpture that today still fill churches, civic buildings, grand palazzi and eventually world-class museums such as the Uffizi Gallery and the Accademia. Architecture prospered here, indeed the city's signature work of art is the masterful Brunelleschi-designed dome of its cathedral, Santa Maria del Fiore, known as the Duomo. The other, has a wonky tower.

BEAUTIFUL FLORENCE

PISA (LEANING TOWER OF)

Local laws in Pisa make it illegal <u>not</u> to hold your hand in the air and have your photograph taken as if you are stopping the tower falling over.

To be fair to Pisa, it is also quite beautiful, the tower being just a part of the The Piazza Dei Miracoli (which means 'field of miracles' or 'field of dreams') The Pizzarians are renowned for their generosity and can often be seen selling designer watches on the street that would cost you thousands of pounds in London, for just a few Euros. This must be because of a local government subsidy which can only be good for attracting tourists into the area.

It is possible to travel to Pisa direct from Livorno by train, but once again, ensure you leave plenty of time to get back to the ship otherwise a lengthy overnight journey to Monte Carlo or Cannes could be on the cards.

From Northern Italy, let's move around the corner into the French Riviera, we'll spend a day berthed at the millionaires playground of Monte Carlo.

Monte Carlo is by any standards, cool, Designer cars parked outside designer boutiques by designer people in designer clothes. The famous Monte Carlo Casino, Cafe de Paris, The Sporting Club and marina. All these places ooze style, sophistication and ultimately, money.

When you leave the ship, you will have to walk through part of the famous marina, past some of the most lavish and expensive yachts that you will see anywhere in the world. Look closer though and you will see that not all is as it seems. The deckhands attentively tying and untying ropes, washing the decks and cutting grapefruits are in fact all played by actors. These have been hired by the boat owners to give the illusion of wealth and importance, look closer still and you will notice that even the most elegant yacht is really just a tarted up trawling vessel that is in port for the day.

'PRIVATE YACHT' IN MONTE CARLO
IS ACTUALLY A SHRIMP BOAT

One of the things Monaco is famous for of course in the Monaco Grand Prix, where the equally filthy rich Formula One brigade come to the Principality for a busman's holiday. The race around the streets is a spectacular sight, tearing around casino square down to the hairpin and through the tunnel to La Rascasse. It is possible to walk the circuit when in town, always remember to make loud engine noises when walking through the tunnel though. Everyone does it and nobody ever laughs at them.

THOUGHT I'D TREAT MYSELF

Also try not to miss out on everyone's favourite pastime here, find the most expensive car around, have your photo taken next to it and put it on Facebook with the quote 'My new car' or 'Thought I'd treat myself' You will be a hero...

Barcelona

Barcelona is an energetic, colourful city where they speak Spanish - a lot. For the cruise passenger, several excursions are available. A trip to see yet another church, you can marvel at the Nou Camp, Barcelona's fantastic modern day place of worship which is a truly magnificent modern arena. Alternatively you can try Las Rambles, the main shopping street with fantastic markets and over 200 stalls selling Barcelona FC woolly scarves (a must in somewhere cold like Spain)

Las Rambles is also the pickpocket capital of the world and I would not be doing this book justice if I didn't offer you some advice on this subject.

1 Stage a fight. The most effective way to steal from somebody is to temporarily divert the person's attention away from his or her belongings. This method requires operating in a group of at least three people. Two of them will pretend to get into a physical fight near the victim while the third will grab the victim's wallet or purse.

2 Use sexuality. One of the most common and effective methods of theft is to use a beautiful woman to distract the target while either she or her partner steals the target's money. In one scenario, the woman may bend down in a revealing outfit in front of the target while another pickpocket steals the wallet from his back pocket. Alternatively, she might do the stealing herself, and distract the target by grabbing him or kissing him, playing off her touches as affection and then secretly grabbing the man's wallet.

3 Take advantage of a good Samaritan. This is perhaps the most ruthless tactic employed by pickpockets, because it preys upon the good nature of the target. Again, this tactic works best in pairs or groups. One person will pretend to be in danger, summoning the attention of the target, while the other steals the money.

Hopefully you will find these tips useful, try not to get caught though as the ship won't wait for you.

FOOD MARKET ON LAS RAMBLES PICKPOCKET'S HEAVEN

Another of the main sights to see in Barcelona is The Cathedral of the Holy Cross and Saint Eulalia. Construction started in the 13th century and continues to this day with the recent addition of huge fake metal cranes which adorn the steepling towers of the building. The cathedral is dedicated to Eulalia of Barcelona, co-patron saint of Barcelona, a young virgin who, according to Catholic tradition, suffered martyrdom during Roman times in the city (Allegedly)

Venice - When cruising to the eastern Med and the Adriatic Sea, no cruise is complete without a visit to Venice.

Venice is off the beaten track and as such, has very few visitors and is among the most inexpensive places in Europe. A couple can have a drink and a bowl of crisps in St Marks Square for less than 200 Euros each, with a live string quartet thrown in for free.

Every November the Venice Town Council flood the square to allow many extra activities for the tourists, you can literally step off of the ship and go swimming, pasta fishing or snorkelling between the tables at Harry's Bar.

MASK SELLERS IN VENICE

Anyone who goes to Venice simply must go on a gondola ride (Cornetto jokes are beneath even me) Your gondondoleer will effortlessly take you from the Grand Canal, under the Rialto bridge with all it's hustle and bustle and into the quiet back streets (canals) of the city.

LIDO DEL ST MARKS

Venice is a city in northeastern Italy sited on a group of 118 small islands separated by canals and linked by bridges. It is located in the marshy Venetian Lagoon which stretches along the shoreline, between the mouths of the Po and the Piave Rivers. Venice is renowned for the beauty of its setting, its architecture and its artworks. The city in its entirety is listed as a

World Heritage Site, along with its lagoon. In peek season, it is estimated that Venice has the highest population density in the world with roughly 9.4 people per square yard. Which explains why it is also called 'The Friendly City'.

VENICE, STRETCHED AND SQUASHED TO FIT THE PAGE

PianO Cruises,

Carnivor House,

22 Crusoe Drive,

Southampton.

SO12 9BE

12th August 2014

Dear Sirs

I am not one who normally complains, I didn't even complain when Waitrose started giving Tesco shoppers free cups of coffee....but I am compelled to write after my experience on The Aramis recently.

When we booked our hard earned cruise (which we paid for by cancelling Sky Sports for six months), we had no idea that our booking was on a timeshare basis and that we would be sharing the room with a little old house proud woman. Although we never saw her, you could guarantee that when we left the room in a right mess, we would come back and the room would be lovely again. At first I thought it might have been my girlfriend but she doesn't do that at home, let alone on holiday. We even had to find excuses to stay out of our room to give the old dear more time. I've never played so much bingo (which can be quite intimidating when you win)....All this should have been explained to us when we booked.

I was shocked and saddened by the prices of the M&Ms in the shop on the Aramis, seriously...I can get them for half the price in Lidl's and I don't even need to sign for them...whilst upsetting, this has given me an idea, how about, on my next cruise, I set up a little market stall in the foyer and sell sweets, books, newspapers and honey?...this would be mutually beneficial and not only could you get rid of that bloke with the peach inspediment in the shop, any money I made would be going straight back to you as I normally lose all my cash playing roulette in the casino.

Is there a rule about not letting Elite passengers have a go at driving the boat?...I repeatedly asked our wine waiter if he could have a word with the captain and get it sorted for me...I wasn't expecting to be able to dock in Venice (not after last time anyway, what a stupid place to park a yacht?) but maybe ten minutes in the Bay of Biscuits couldn't have hurt?...this really upset me, so much so that we started going to the buffet for dinner. If there isn't a rule about this and it was just the captain being awkward, please let me know what disciplinary measures you intend to take against him and the rest of his staff. As a victim, maybe I could suggest a keelhauling for a first offence with a dozen lashes with the cat o nine tails for further infringements?

Now this isn't a complaint but just a few suggestions to make the cruises more fun for people. As exciting as the art auctions are, not many of us have the odd £20 grand hanging about, so I suggest we scrap those and start mobility scooter racing around the prom deck. We can still incorporate the free champagne from the art auctions and I think that would just add to the fun!...I would be happy to run a book on the races and pay you a cut (we could just keep this between ourselves) Another idea I had is 'knock down ginger' honestly, with so many cabins and doors we could have a right laugh, I reckon 6.00am would be a good time to knock on doors and run away as some people might want to be up by then anyway.

It's funny being on a cruise because everyone has a different accent and some of them come from outside the home counties so we can't really understand them...but it would be good fun, if say, for one day, everyone has to speak with a Welsh accent?...it would be brilliant 'Hello isn't it didn't I mun'...nobody could not enjoy that!

I have attached a further list of complaints for your attention, please read them carefully and don't even try to fob me off with a free 100 day world cruise (in a suite) because I cannot be bought (cheaply)

Yours faithfully

Graham Clifford

PIANO CRUISES
Discover a world of indifference...

20th August 2014

Our ref: DT16/477

Dear Mr Clifford

Thank you for your letter dated 12th August 2014 which has been passed on to me for consideration.

Your list of complaints and recommendations stretched to several pages so perhaps we can look at each item in turn:

Item 1) Please be assured that your cabin on the Aramis was solely for your use and was not by any means a 'timeshare' with someone else using it while you were playing bingo. I understand your concerns that you left the room in a 'right mess' and when you returned everything was 'lovely' again. This would have been entirely due to your cabin steward who's role it is, among other duties, to keep your stateroom clean and definitely not 'some little old woman' who moved in when your were out.

Item 2) At PianO Cruises we pride ourselves on our commitment to our passengers and endeavour to keep our prices low at bars, shops and boutiques throughout our fleet. Whilst we appreciate that you can purchase a large bag of M&M's at Lidl's for half the price that you paid in our shop, please understand the logistical arrangements involved in delivering and selling items at sea are complex and in turn our prices accurately reflect the cost's involved. Under no circumstances can we allow you to 'set up a stall' in the foyer and undercut our prices to fund your roulette habit.

Item 3) You will be aware that in these modern times, ship security and the safety of our passengers must be our over riding priority. I understand that you repeatedly requested that your wine waiter ask the Captain if you can 'have a go' at driving the ship. Whilst we regret that this was not possible, we will not be taking any disciplinary action against the Captain or any of his staff...and they will certainly not be 'keelhauled'.

Item 4) Whilst we here at PianO believe we have a great sense of fun, your suggestion of mobility scooter races around the Promenade deck is a non starter – as are the 'knock down ginger' and the 'get everyone to speak Welsh for a day' competitions.

Thank you for taking the trouble to write to us here at PianO, I hope I have managed to explain our position on your comments clearly and look forward to your future bookings with PianO Cruises.

Yours sincerely

Richard Cooper

PianO Cruises, Carnivor House, 22 Crusoe Drive, Southampton. SO12 9BE

Tel: 0842 911 470 Fax: 0842 911 475   Registered in England 909172638909

FOA Richard Cooper
PianO Cruises
Carnivor House
22 Crusoe Drive
Southampton
SO12 9BE

15th September 2014

Hi Rich

Thanks for your reply after my letter about the Aramis expedition, I took some of the things you said onboard.

I have just returned from another expedition on behalf of PianO, this time on the Naultilis(how do you think up these names?!?)

As you probably know by now, I am an international superstar on the PianO Facebook page with fans from places like Bournemouth and as far as Bognor Regis. Giving my status, I think the only way to describe our arrival at the cruise terminal in Southampton is below par. We were treated like ordinary passengers, forced to stand in line and believe it or not, not one of your staff recognised either my tropical Hawaiian shirt or myself. Richie, if we are to remain penpals, this needs addressing. Even when I shouted 'Don't you know who I think I am' - all I received from your staff was looks of derision...perhaps an internal memo should be sent out to all PianO employees prior to my next sailing?

Having spoken to your onboard staff in the past and heard their terrible tales of suffering and woe, we decided to book an inside hutch this time, in order to donate more money to the poor under-developed photographers who remind me of something from a zombie apocalypse (for goodness sake man, let them sleep now and then) Anyway, our inside hutch...upon inspection these hutches are maybe 10 feet wide but they go on forever and ever!...each portion is separated though and I was dismayed to see dodgy looking geezers in every single compartment, I don't think they noticed me (two way glass?) I was saddened one evening to notice my girlfriend in one of the other compartments of our hutch in SOMEONE ELSE'S BED wearing her Scooby Do pyjamas - she denied it of course so we had an impromptu ice bucket challenge on deck the next morning.

I think I may have been a victim of one of your (now) infamous pranks?...On the first full day I attended what I was led to believe was a fancy dress get together for members of the PianO cruises facebook page - I like to think I am a good sport but can you imagine my embarrassment when I turned up as Father Christmas and everyone was in their normal 'Oompa Loompa cloths' (Spray tan is a terrible thing)

I was particularly dismayed at the growing numbers of marauding grannies who terrorise the buffet from 7.00am until 7.00pm...I witnessed a 25 stone man from Wales being hurled over the salad bar, children kicked and some of them even tasted the soup by dunking their teeth into it. Seriously Rich, you need to look at this otherwise people will stop eating the free food at the buffet and will start eating at the premium restaurants ⊗

We started our cruise on a Sunday and I was keen to watch the Headliners show in the Playhouse Theatre, being on the grown ups 8.30pm dinner sitting however, by the time our waiter Silvano had explained the following days breakfast arrangements, we found that the theatre was full. This happened again the next evening so I, showing some initiative, decided to put a towel on a seat to ensure I could see the show. Would you believe, someone removed to towel (and my book) and left them by the entrance??? - how rude. Not being put off by this however, I noticed a spare seat on the stage, it appears one of the band was late so I thought it would help us both out (I used to play the brass blowy thing anyway) I must say, your Ninja security team are good though, I was offstage before you could say Llanfairpwllgwyngyllgogerychwyrndrobwllllantysiliogogogoch.

On another occasion, my Gazpacho 'soup' was cold so I asked Silvano if he would pop it in the microwave, once again I was disappointed...

Was it a coincidence that in my last letter, I spoke of opening a stall in the atrium to sell cut price M&Ms...next thing I know, everyone else on our table is being served with their beef Wellington whilst I get a plate of peanut M&Ms and a rather clever napkin rose? Captain Dembridge mucking around maybe?

Contact details, evidential photographs and a separate list of irritations attached...are you on Twitter?

Hoping for a speedy reply

Many thanks

Graham Clifford

PIANO CRUISES
Discover a world of indifference...

16th September 2014

Dear Mr Clifford

Thank you for your letter dated 15th September, I hope this response is 'speedy' enough for you.

As a valued customer, we welcome your comments regarding your recent cruise on the Nautilus. We would however prefer you to refer to it as your holiday, rather than 'another research expedition on behalf of PianO'

Once again, let's deal with your comments individually:

Item 1) I am sorry to hear that your reception at Southampton was 'below par' I understand your celebrity status on the PianO Facebook page but please understand that we treat all our customers on an equal basis and as we have an enormous client base, it would be impossible for our staff to recognise either you, or your tropical Hawaiian shirt. The fact that you had to walk through the terminal in relative obscurity is regrettable but shouting 'Don't you know who I think I am' to our operators is unacceptable.

Item 2) You state that you 'opted for an inside Hutch' so that you would have more money to donate to our photographers...but were surprised how big the 'hutch' was? Mr Hampsheir, please be assured that the 'hutch' didn't have one way glass which looked into several rooms with 'dodgy looking geezers' – all our inside staterooms have large mirrors on opposing walls which are intended to maximise the artificial light – I hope this averts your fears and convinces you that you didn't see your girlfriend wearing Scooby Do pyjamas in someone else's bed.

Item 3) I can honestly say that I wasn't behind the prank to get you to go to a Facebook cruisers meeting in a Father Christmas outfit. Perhaps you should look closer to home?

Item 4) As far as I know, PianO are not aware or 'gangs of marauding Grannies' terrorising the buffet, pushing people out of the way, kicking children or dunking their teeth in the soup. If you have any evidence of this, please send it to me.

Item 5) I have been informed by our Entertainment Manager that your towel was removed from the seat in the Playhouse theatre. I appreciate that you were upset that you couldn't get a seat for the previous two evenings but we have a strict 'no reservation' policy. On a more serious note, trying to sit with the band during live shows is also very much frowned upon, no matter how good you are at the 'brass blowy thing'

Item 6) Gazpacho soup is supposed to be cold...

I have noted your other comments and will reply when I have further investigated the matter. But in the meantime, I am not sure how Captain Dembridge saw your previous letter but I can assure you that he didn't arrange the plate of M&Ms instead of the Beef Wellington for you.

Yours sincerely

Richard Cooper

PianO Cruises, Carnivor House, 22 Crusoe Drive, Southampton. SO12 9BE
Tel: 0842 911 470 Fax: 0842 911 475   Registered in England 909172638909

ABTA
ABTA No 03927a

20) Cruise lines & ships

The cruising industry is massive, more and more of us are choosing to spend our holidays on floating towns with everything you need in one place.

With demand at record highs, supply is plentiful with a huge choice of cruise lines and ships. Let's have a look at what is available:

Currently, the largest cruise ships in the world are Royal Caribbean's Allure of the Seas and her sister ship Oasis of the Seas. Both weigh in at 225,000 tonnes and are the length of four football pitches and as wide as one also.

ALLURE OF THE SEAS COMPARED TO THE TITANIC

It is estimated that seventeen of the three thousand people who built the Allure are still onboard somewhere, living homeless and being moved on from lifeboat to lifeboat. Some have resorted to begging in the main high street, some have become buskers who can often be seen plying their trade in theatres and lounges throughout the ship.

The Allure relentlessly travels the seas and oceans of the world and calls at many countries. As you can imagine, the ship's size brings it's own problems. On a recent visit to Southampton, millions of tonnes of extra water were brought into the Solent to ensure that it didn't bottom out.

The logistics for a ship of this size are immense, at the start of a 14 day cruise, the following is taken onboard:

12,000 live chickens

600 cows

4000 fishing rods

30.000 bottles of champagne

1.4 million peas

1 bow tie

80,000 eggs

50,000 bottles of beer

5000 Yukka plants

1200 pigs

10,000 oranges

12,000 bottles of 'Blue Nun'

3 tonnes of potatoes

and a jar of Marmite.

CAPTAINS QUARTERS

At the other end of the scale however, things are very different, on the smaller ships for example, all that is required is a bottle of sherry, a white sliced loaf and a jar of pickles.

There are many cruise lines these days, Cunard, Royal Caribbean, Princess, P&O, Holland America, to name a few. The ships visit every continent on Earth and accommodate millions of customers every year. In a world dictated to by supply and demand, cruise companies and ship designers are looking at ever innovative ways of attracting new customers. At present on a cruise ship, you can go ice skating, slide through a water flume around a ship, play golf at St Andrews and order drinks from a robot.

Soon the following will be available:

Under water viewing platform - watch dolphins and whales in their natural environment from the vast (50 feet x 10 feet) windows below the water line.

Sea view: The North Star glass pod on Quantum of the Seas
(Picture: Royal Caribbean)

The Quantum of Seas has a glass pod in which passengers can be raised 300 feet above the waves, best experienced in the Bay of Biscay in a force 10 gale.

Para gliding will be introduced off of the stern of some of the larger ships, extra long cables will allow the hardy participants to fly up to two miles up in the air and will be propelled along at 22 knots.

Mobility scooter racing is becoming increasingly popular, at present there are only unofficial races that take place between the main dining rooms and the theatre after dinner. There are plans however for new ships to have dedicated race tracks around deck 6 with banked curves. chicanes and an independent electricity supply. This is set to be the next big thing on ships, bookmakers will take bets and passengers will be able to watch the races from the prom deck and even take charge of the scooters with Scalextric style controllers. This is very exciting!

BARRY & COLIN IN QUALIFYING

It seems that most of the technology in Star Trek eventually becomes a reality and that has never been more true than than in the new classes of ships being developed. Boffins at S.O.D.S (Society Of Ship Designers) are working on a fusion reactor that when combined with Piña Coladas will generate warp speed. This is still quite a way off as early tests have resulted in ships leaving Fort Lauderdale and arriving in Southampton 3 days before they left meaning the ships weren't in Fort Lauderdale to start with. Such are the intricacies of time travel.

All ships from 2022 onwards will be fitted with a holodeck (which also doesn't appear in spellcheck) Passengers will be able to visit a pre set world and act out various scenarios. You could be in the band on the Titanic, witness the invention of the telephone or see what really happened on the first cruise ship 'Noahs Ark'

All this is happening, it's true and it looks like a fantastic period for cruisers. Some other ideas are being bandied around but to my mind, seem a bit far fetched:

Room to turn around in showers...

Enough tables in buffet dining rooms...

Less cruise brochures through the post...

Free wifi for everyone...

Royal Caribbean are often at the forefront of design innovations, another one of their's is the introduction of virtual balconies. The virtual balconies will be 80-inch LED projection screen that stretches from floor to ceiling. They offer digital real-time views of the ocean and destinations visible from the ship's exterior.

It is displayed in high-resolution colour on a giant 80-inch LED screen on the wall of an otherwise windowless stateroom. It will work at sea and in port, just don't stick your head through it.

INSIDE STATEROOM WITH VIRTUAL BALCONY

Photo: Royal Caribbean

Not for the faint hearted is the Seawalk on the Regal Princess. This glass bottomed walkway extends out from the ship and seems to float 130 feet above the sea. Ladies are requested not to wear dresses or skirts when using the Seawalk as it does attract keen photographers from the promenade deck seventy feet below.

21) Dress codes

Dress code is important on a cruise, it's what distinguishes us from savages (in most cases) Let's have a look at how this works.

Boarding: When travelling to your ship, comfort is probably the most important thing. For men It seems sandals (with socks) cargo shorts and a short sleeve shirt three sizes to small. These along with a rucksack and a brand new Panama hat from M&S seem to be the norm. Ladies generally opt for summer dresses with flat sandals and a carry on bag the size of a lama.

When safely boarded, the only time you really need to fit in with the dress code is in the evenings, even then though, it is not compulsory but you will get turned away from the dining rooms if you turn up in a skimpy bikini gentlemen.

Dress codes vary from cruise line to cruise line. Generally speaking though, they are: Black-tie, smart and evening casual nights. Black-tie attire includes a dinner jacket or tuxedo (or, alternatively, dark suit or kilt and jacket) for men and a ball gown, trouser suit or cocktail dress for women. Smart attire includes jacket and tie for men and anything from tailored trousers to smart separates or an elegant dress for women. Casual attire includes open-neck or polo shirts and trousers or smart jeans for men and casual separates, dresses or smart jeans for women.

The main dress codes are:

Casual

Semi Casual

Formal (Black tie)

Black & White

1980s

Tropical

Semi tropical

FORMAL

SEMI CASUAL

BLACK & WHITE

TROPICAL

80s NIGHT

CENSORED

CASUAL

22) Captain & Staff

With the exception of the cocktail/ice crushing machines, the most important attribute to a cruise ship are the staff. With a customer/crew ratio of three to one and some of the largest ships carrying over 6000 passengers, the ships company can be huge.

The captain is God on a ship. What he says goes, and if he doesn't like your bow tie, you had better go and change it, such are the powers of the man. Captains tend to be portrayed as happy, jovial people with a great sense of humour. But underneath this exterior is a man of steel, a serious, confident man who knows his stuff. Lets face it, we want him to be serious, he is driving a 200,000 tonne floating city around the world, navigating narrow passes and gently docking this huge beast in tight docks, ports and marinas - this is not a position to be filled by Woody Allen.

Lets have a look at the hierarchy at sea:

Captain/Master - The guv'nor, the boss, Capo di tutti cap (Boss of bosses) The main man, in charge of everything and everyone on the ship. Generally nice people who are natural achievers in life. Steadfast and reassuringly in control. Pretty much not silly at all (on duty)

(The Captain is the highest ranking officer and the Master of the cruise ship. He/she has a full authority to make executive decisions in order to preserve the life and safety of the ship's personnel and guest and must apply extreme care and proper judgement according to any given situation)

Staff Captain - In Star Trek terms, the Staff Captain is the Captains Number One, his 'go to' man. The ships assistant boss needs to know everything about the Federation of Planets, warp drive and Klingon cloaking devices. Quite important.

(The Staff Captain is the second in command aboard the cruise ship and Head of the Deck Department. Must be familiar with all duties and responsibilities of the Master and should be able to assume command of the vessel at any time.)

1st Officer - The 1st Officer is like the school prefect, always sucking up to the senior officers but never quite being part of their club. Takes everything seriously in an effort to be noticed by the Captain. Works long hours and terrorises those beneath him/her.

(The 1st Officer is a bridge Watch keeper (Officer of the Watch or OOW) and on behalf of the Master is responsible for all navigational and watch keeping issues)

2nd Officer - Responsible for polishing the 1st Officers shoes, ironing their shirts and basically do all the running around that the 1st Officer is supposed to be doing. They often hide in the ships laundry room and try to look busy at all times. Has the privilege of being allowed on the bridge but is generally bullied by the bigger boys and is a figure of fun and the victim of cruel pranks.

(The 2nd Officer is a Navigation and Watch Keeping Officer and Bridge Team Member. Reports to the Master and to the Staff Captain. During his/her watch the 2nd Officer is representing the Master and is in command on the bridge. Responsible for the safe navigation of the vessel. During the watch adheres to the emergency procedures and monitors bridge equipment and watertight doors status.)

3rd Officer - Ironically, the 3rd Officer is unofficially senior to the 2nd Officer. The 3rd Officer is respected on the bridge and spoken to with respect by everybody. This of course is just to wind up the 2nd Officer who cannot understand why his deputy is part of the clique that he/she is so desperate wants to join.

(The Third Officer is an assistant to the OOW or the Junior Watch Keeping Officer on the ship. Reports to the Officer of the Watch (either 1st or 2nd Officer) for navigation and watch keeping aspects and to the Staff Captain for all other issues. Acts as a co-navigator on bigger ships, on smaller vessels could perform OOW functions during a day time as delegated by the Master)

Safety Officer - Roles include putting out signs saying 'Caution, wet floor', stopping speeding mobility scooters and generally fussing over everyone and everything. Scared of their own shadows, these delicate people see danger in everything and would see everyone confined to their staterooms should the ship encounter anything above 1 foot swells and 6 inch wavelets. Not popular on the bridge thanks to quotes such as 'Ooh Captain, that coffee looks too hot' 'Have we got enough petrol' and 'MIND THAT ROCK!'

(The Safety Officer is responsible for passenger and crew safety drills, abandon ship procedures, crew safety training, supervision of ships tenders, instructions on safety of all shipboard personnel, with particular reference to emergency procedures, fire fighting and the accident prevention program)

Environmental Compliance Officer - The ECO is basically just a clerk, hated by senior bridge officers and often sent to spend their days being dragged in an inflatable dingy off of the stern of the ship looking for anything that may have been thrown overboard. An intelligent person, the ECO is responsible for reading mountains of regulations that contain long words such as 'Environmentalism, 'Implementationalism' and 'Decognacomplianteenial' (I'm surprised spellcheck didn't pick up on that one...but it didn't!?!)

The ECO (or just EO) is a three-stripe, non-watch standing officer responsible for oversight and verification of the cruise line environmental policies, the training, implementation, and verification of regulatory compliance as it relates to applicable environmental laws. The EO reports directly to the Staff Captain.

Chief Security Officer - Normally ex-SAS, these are the guys that even the head chef won't argue with. Especially trained to stop drug trafficking, terrorists and pirates, they spend most of their time confiscating cigarettes and alcohol from pubescent 14 year old boys who are desperately trying to impress the girls. In between arresting drunken travellers and warning dolphins not to get too close to the ship, Chief Security Officers can often be seen in the crew bar talking about their exploits in the Falklands or Bosnia. Some CSO's work undercover and as such could be anyone, they rarely dress a Nuns however but that doesn't mean that they don't.

(The Chief Security Officer is a three-stripe officer who is in charge of implementing the company security policies and all security operations on board the cruise ship both at sea and while in port. He/she must be professionally trained security expert, familiar with illegal drugs trafficking and anti-terrorist countermeasures)

Quartermaster - There are four quartermasters on a cruise ship (obviously) When these four all agree with each other on an issue, only the Captain can over rule them, and even then he needs backing from either 8 waiters, 4 entertainment staff or the man who goes around touching up the prom deck with his little pot of white paint.

(The Quartermaster (QM), also named Helmsman is an unlicensed member of the deck crew, an Able Seaman who is performing also Bridge Watch Keeping duties. The main duties and responsibilities of the Quartermaster include, but are not limited to:

Reports to the Bosun (Boatswain)

Performs Watch Keeping duties on the bridge and steers the ship applying the helm orders given by the Officer of the Watch (OOW)

Stands watch also as a Lookout, observing the sea for potential hazards, other ships, floating objects, icebergs, land, etc. and reporting any changes to the OOW)

CSO Chris McNab - or is it?

Able Seaman - By definition, the Able Seaman is not, unable. In fact the position of Unable Seaman isn't really recognised in either the Royal Navy, or the Merchant Navy. So using the word 'Able' is superfluous to requirements. This has annoyed me a bit, you don't get Able Waiters, Able Engineers or Able Spa Ladies, so why Able Seaman? Grrrr.

(The Able Seaman (AB) is a non-officer member of the deck crew (deck rating position). The main duties and responsibilities of the AB include:

Reporting to the Bosun (Boatswain)

Performing a variety of routine maintenance duties in order to preserve the painted surface of the ship such as chipping, cleaning, painting and removing rust spots from deck and sides of ship using hand or air chipping hammer and wire brush. Responsibility for keeping the vessel in a clean, tidy condition.)

23) Oddities

Cruise passengers can be a fickle lot, they can ask a lot of pertinent questions, but here are some genuine, not so clever questions asked on a cruise ship:

Do these steps go up or down?

Who steers the ship at night?

Wouldn't it just be safer to anchor in bad weather? (on an Atlantic crossing)

Is the water in the Caribbean sea, fresh or sea water?

What do you do with the beautiful ice carvings after they melt?

Do the value of the casino chips change when we go to a foreign country?

Which elevator do I take to get to the front of the ship?

How far away from the horizon are we at the moment?

Does the crew sleep on the ship?

Can I use my cruise card ashore?

Which deck is number seven?

What deck will my car be on and can I get it off at the ports?

Can I smoke in the shower?

Is this island completely surrounded by water?

Can I fish from the prom deck?

Does the ship make its own electricity?

Is it salt water in the toilets?

What elevation are we at?

There's a team of photographers on board who take photos and display them, next day... the question asked...If the pictures aren't marked, how will I know which ones are mine?

What time is the Midnight Buffet being served?

24) Elevators

Elevators on a ship are quite unlike any others anywhere. there are many unwritten rules for these vertical personal transporters, the sooner you understand how they work on your cruise, the better.

Rule 1) Lifts are a luxury, not a right. Just because you need to go up nine decks, it would be wrong of you to expect a lift to take you there. Please understand that there are people who need to go down one level and their need is obviously more important.

2) The more desperate you are to get to your chosen deck, the slower the lift will move, and it will stop on every floor and the doors will take an age to close, even when Ethel from deck 5 keeps pushing the 'close doors' button (which turns out to be the 'keep doors open' button.

3) When asked what floor you want, always say 13 or 23, this amusing little prank never fails to get a laugh.

4) If you should travel in a packed elevator in total silence, always be polite and say 'Thank you' when you leave. It's expected and frowned upon when it doesn't happen.

5) Elevator chat should be limited to the following: 'Going up?', 'What floor would you like?', 'Ooh I like your dress', and 'Did you see the comedian tonight?'

6) The best place for your gaze is either at the numbers of the floors, or your own feet.

7) Do not stand near the buttons unless you are willing and able to operate the door close/door open buttons like a pro. The door close button is of almost sacred importance, as it helps quicken the journey and can be used to great satisfaction to shut out a running Johnny-Come-Lately.

8) When children enter the elevator, they must immediately start making hands prints on all the mirrors. Failure to do so can result in job losses for the cleaners so this is most important.

9) When exiting an elevator, etiquette dictates that you must first go left, then 10 seconds later return and go right. Elevators doors are especially designed to stay open for this to ensure everyone sees you doing this. Chuckles and giggles are short lived however as they all do it on their respective decks.

Elevators on P&O's Azura go to deck ninety-six apparently. When asked about this, P&O said it was a technical fault. That is possible but a more likely explanation is that deck ninety-six is a bit like platform 9¾ in the Harry Potter books, whereby aspiring ship Captains can enrol at Ropetaughts School of Captaincy. Probably.

25) Cruise terminology

If you should join an online cruise forum, you will initially be confused by the jargon they use, lets try to explain:

OH – 'Other half'

OBC – 'On board credit'

MDR – Main dining room

DOD – Drink of the Day

FCC – Future Cruise Credit

ES – Early Saver

DD– Darling daughter

DS – Darling son

WTC – Where's the Captain?

WTD – What time's dinner?

FOB – Friends of Bill W (Don't know)

FOD – Friends of Dorothy (Wizard of Oz fan group)

GLBT – Great lettuce, bacon & tomato (Sandwich)

CD – Cruise director (or cross dresser, or both)

B2B – Back to back cruises

TDSM – That doesn't make sense

HYFINB – Have you finished in the bathroom

OKIGTGTTBWYFGR – Ok, I'm going to go to the bar while you finish getting ready

YCTSIISTLORDY – You checked to see if I spelt that last one right didn't you?

IYGBTTRCYGMBP – If you are going back to the room, can you get my book please?

IRCUWTUSMAOCS – I really can't understand why they use so many acronyms on cruise ships

Elderly passengers on a ship have their own acronyms which they tend to keep secret - we have discovered the following though:

ATD: At The Doctor's

BTW: Bring The Wheelchair

BYOT: Bring Your Own Teeth

CBM: Covered By Medicare

DWI: Driving While Incontinent

FWB: Friend With Beta Blockers

FWIW: Forgot Where I Was

FYI: Found Your Insulin

GGPBL: Gotta Go Pacemaker Battery Low

GHA: Got Heartburn Again

HGBM: Had Good Bowel Movement

IMHO: Is My Hearing-Aid On?

LMDO: Laughing My Dentures Out

OMMR: On My Massage Recliner

ROFL... CGU: Rolling On The Floor Laughing... And Can't Get Up

TTYL: Talk To You Louder

WAITT: Who Am I Talking To?

WTFA: Wet The Furniture Again

WTP: Where's The Prunes?

WWNO: Walker Wheels Need Oil

LMGA: Lost My Glasses Again

GLKI (Gotta Go, Laxative Kicking In)

26) The Gym

One of the most eagerly awaited and then seldom used facilities on a ship is the gym. For months before your cruise you plan to be sensible this time, your not going to eat and drink too much and you are going to go to the gym every day.

This is unlikely to happen however unless they have renamed the Crooners Bar 'THE GYM'. Despite your best made plans, it's not going to happen, sure you may go into the gym and have a look around but unless you are a regular gym goer at home, the lure of everything else on the ship will keep you away.

I would urge you to stay away from the gym in any case. It has been a closely guarded secret for years by the major cruise companies, that this unassuming sweatshop on the ships in fact saves them millions of pounds a year in running costs. For every treadmill, cross trainer and exercise bike are connected up to the ships generator system and in total supply approximately 20% of the power needed to run the ship. Ever wondered why it is free to use the gym?...now you know.

Auxiliary power units on The Oasis of the Seas provide over 10,000 kilowatts of extra electricity

If you should venture into the gym, you will see the following people: The ship's dancers, Big Dan from Dagenham, Mr & Mrs Sensible from Surbiton, 30 stone Peter who has never seen a gym in his life but is amazed by all the lights on the treadmills, the 2nd Officer trying to impress the Captain & 1st Officer (and failing), two ladies who met at second dinner sitting who have planned to go everyday but will give up by day 4.

27) The Laundrette

The laundrette is the social hub of a cruise ship. Here you will find all kinds of characters, the obsessive machine hoggers, the OCD ironers, the laundry virgins and people who want to get away from all the 'poshness' and back to civvy street.

Machine hoggers are among the rudest people that you will ever meet. They will remove people's clothes from washers and dryers and throw it on the floor, take up 3 ironing boards with their bags of dirty washing and generally treat the place like they own it. (a small bottle of red food colouring in their wash normally brings them down to ground)

The OCD ironers are a band women who tend to live in the laundry, they speak in their own language and are quite jovial. Get on the right side of one of these expert laundrarians and you can get your clothes expertly ironed at no cost.

Laundry virgins, by definition, have never used one in their lives, it is a novel experience for them and the whole thing can be daunting. Where do they get powder?. How much are the machines? How long does the dryer take? They will often spend a whole day trying to do their washing and will end up with some clean but damp items which they need to wear to dinner in 30 minutes.

When is the right time to use the laundry? - Generally when you have clothes that you want cleaning as a rule. There are however, good and bad times to use the facilities. Late on in a cruise on a sea day can be a nightmare, everyone has the same idea and the room can be busier than the ship's reception desk when passengers have heard that someone has popped their clogs and and balcony stateroom has just become available.

The best time to use the laundry is probably when it opens at 7.30am although to stand a chance of getting a machine, you probably need to camp in the corridor from around 10.00pm the evening before along with the OCD ironers.

Alternatively, if you don't want to do your own washing, all ships offer a laundry service, all items have different prices and you are assured of a thorough cleaning by the professionals who work from a wooden platform just outside deck one.

28) Internet forums

When planning your first cruise, you may decide to look online for information. Naturally there are many web sites where cruise companies will ply their trade and try to convince you that they have the perfect solution for you.

It may be better to look at independent forums for impartial information. There is a huge choice out there and you will discover the truth about cruising rather than just what the cruise companies want you to know. Be warned though, there is a huge turf war going on with the privately run forums, and there are inevitable casualties. This occurs when someone joins opposing groups and the administrators find out. Say the wrong thing and you will be vaporised instantly by some egotistic anti-Christ with delusions of grandeur. I speak from experience!

There are two kinds of people on these pages, those who enjoy life and have fun, and those who take literally everything seriously. Trying to convince someone that you don't really mean the captain should be keelhauled or that you don't really want to open an M&M outlet in the atrium can be an uphill battle.

Make sure when you join a forum that you asked inane questions like 'Are there hangers in the wardrobes?' 'Do they do decaffeinated coffee in the buffet?' Or flirt with danger and ask 'Can I smoke in the main dining room?' (World War III will erupt). These tedious questions get asked again and again and even the most harmless question can set an argument rolling which will result in several people being banished from the group.

The best way not to get thrown out of an online cruise page is to not comment, just join, lurk in the shadows and observe from a distance. If you do post however, ensure you post at least 200 cruise photo's on there, there will be many experts on hand to tell you what you did wrong and offer unwanted advice on what aperture settings, shutter speeds and selective focus you should have used.

Emma Wyeth

2hrs

Totally serious question, we are going on our first cruise next month and someone said we can't take our car onboard despite the fact that the agency we booked through said we would have free parking - does this sound right?

Pauline Traynor

2hrs

That's terrible Emma, who did you book with? We always take our car onboard, we were allowed to park ours on our balcony and it is craned off at every port.

Pat Sunderland

2hrs

Why aye pet, who said you couldn't take it onboard?

Steven Blackpool

2hrs

They mean you get free parking at the port Emma, it's a cruise ship, not a ferry. Only the Captain can park onboard.

Brian 'Wat' Tyler

1hr

Why can't you just answer her seriously, it was a straight forward question and there was no need for any micky taking. Although you got free parking Emma, sometimes, particularly on a long cruise, they cannot accommodate everyone because they need more room for the livestock.

John Dubrovnic

1hr

What part of Sunderland are you from Pat?

Pat Sunderland

1hr

I'm not from Sunderland John, that's my surname, what part of John are you from?

Drew Peacock (Admin)

20 mins

Unless this nonsense stops you will all be deleted from this page. We run a serious page about cruising. We are not here for fun or to enjoy ourselves so if you don't like it, go away, go on, leave now. Right that's it, you are all expelled. Just leave me alone here on MY PAGE, THAT'S RIGHT, MY PAGE.

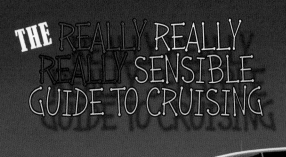

THE REALLY REALLY REALLY SENSIBLE GUIDE TO CRUISING

Dear Reader
Many thanks for buying this book, it was suggested and inspired by some wonderful people on a cruise forum who shared my sense of humour (seriously!)
I hope you have enjoyed reading about cruising, please remember that the book is, for the most part, a tongue in cheek look at cruising and shouldn't be taken too seriously. Cruising is a fantastic way to spend your holiday/vacation (had to say vacation because I have sold a copy in the USA) You will have a fantastic time, eat fabulous food and meet some charming people. Enjoy your cruise!

Many thanks

Graham Clifford

Printed in Great Britain
by Amazon.co.uk, Ltd.,
Marston Gate.